11/13/14

The BOSTON MASSACRE

By Therese Shea

Gareth Stevens
Publishing

Please visit our website, www.garethstevens.com. For a free color catalog of all our high-quality books, call toll free 1-800-542-2595 or fax 1-877-542-2596.

Library of Congress Cataloging-in-Publication Data

Shea, Therese M.
The Boston Massacre / by Therese M. Shea.
 p. cm. — (What you didn't know about history)
Includes index.
ISBN 978-1-4824-3328-9 (pbk.)
ISBN 978-1-4824-3329-6 (6-pack)
ISBN 978-1-4824-0580-4 (library binding)
1. Boston Massacre, 1770 — Juvenile literature. I. Shea, Therese. II. Title.
E215.4 S54 2014
973.3'113—dc23

First Edition

Published in 2014 by
Gareth Stevens Publishing
111 East 14th Street, Suite 349
New York, NY 10003

Copyright © 2014 Gareth Stevens Publishing

Designer: Andrea Davison-Bartolotta
Editor: Kristen Rajczak

Photo credits: Cover, p. 1 Prisma/UIG/Getty Images; pp. 5, 14 Hulton Archive/Getty Images; p. 7 Mansell/Time & Life Pictures/Getty Images; pp. 8, 13 (main), 19 MPI/Getty Images; p. 9 Kean Collection/Getty Images; p. 10 iStockphoto/Thinkstock; p. 11 © iStockphoto.com/ WilshireImages; p. 13 (inset) New York Public Library/Photo Researchers/Getty Images; p. 15 courtesy of Wikimedia Commons; p. 17 Stock Montage/Getty Images; p. 20 Roel Smart/E+/Getty Images.

Printed in the United States of America

CPSIA compliance information: Batch #CW14GS: For further information contact Gareth Stevens, New York, New York at 1-800-542-2595.

CONTENTS

Before the Revolution............................4

Taxes and Soldiers...............................6

Calling for Help.................................8

Bayonets and Snowballs........................10

Crispus Attucks................................12

The Trials.....................................14

Who Said "Fire"?...............................16

The Soldiers' Trial.............................18

After the Massacre.............................20

Glossary......................................22

For More Information...........................23

Index 24

Words in the glossary appear in **bold** type the first time they are used in the text.

BEFORE THE REVOLUTION

You probably know a lot about the American **Revolution**. In 1776, 13 British colonies declared their independence from England. Against all odds, they won their freedom. But what happened to make the colonists angry with England in the first place?

In March 1770, 5 years before the Battles of Lexington and Concord, **violence** broke out in Massachusetts between colonists and British soldiers. The event became known as the Boston **Massacre**. What do a wig and snowballs have to do with this famous event? Read on to find out!

Did You Know?

No one knows who fired the first shot of the American Revolution.

Colonists and British soldiers fought near Lexington and Concord in Massachusetts on April 19, 1775. These were the first battles of the American Revolution.

TAXES AND SOLDIERS

It wasn't just one event that led to the violence in Boston, Massachusetts. Anger had been growing for years. England had let the colonies govern themselves for a long time. However, after the French and Indian War (1754–1763), the British government needed money to pay off **debts**. They collected some of that money by taxing the colonies.

England taxed paper, sugar, and other products. Many colonists believed it was unfair since they didn't have **representation** in British government.

Did You Know?

The Boston Massacre wasn't the first time the colonists and British soldiers clashed. Just 3 days before, a group of rope makers and soldiers had fought.

This image shows how some colonists reacted after the Stamp Act was passed in 1765.

CALLING FOR HELP

On the night of March 5, wigmaker's **apprentice** Edward Garrick (sometimes called Gerrish) accused a British officer of not paying his master for a wig. Another British soldier, who was guarding government offices on King Street, replied that the officer was a gentleman and would pay him. Garrick then **insulted** the soldier. He said none of the British soldiers were gentlemen!

The soldier lost his temper and struck the young man with his gun. Garrick yelled for help. Soon, a crowd grew around the soldier.

British soldier

In 1770, many colonists in Boston were still angry about the taxes. Others disliked the soldiers because they often worked low-paying part-time jobs in the city, which took jobs from colonists.

Did You Know?

About 4,000 troops were sent to Boston in 1768 to make sure the colonists were obeying British laws. That seemed like a lot to many colonists, since Boston's population was only about 20,000 at that time.

BAYONETS AND SNOWBALLS

Worried the crowd would harm the soldier, British captain Thomas Preston arrived at the scene with several more men. The crowd increased, yelling and waving clubs and sticks. Someone even rang a loud fire bell!

The mob screamed at the British soldiers, calling them "lobsters" because of their red coats. The angry people closed in on the armed soldiers, coming as close as the tips of their **bayonets**! They threw huge snowballs, chunks of ice, oyster shells, and rocks.

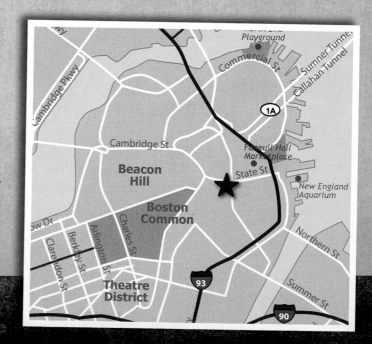

★ location of the Boston Massacre

This star in Boston marks the place where the events of the Boston Massacre occurred. Some accounts say there may have been hundreds of colonists in the angry crowd that night.

Did You Know?

Some colonists in the crowd dared the soldiers to fire!

CRISPUS ATTUCKS

Then, a heavy club hit one of the soldiers. He fell, and a yell was heard: "Fire!" The first colonist killed was a former slave named Crispus Attucks. About eight shots rang out—but no one knows the number for sure.

Some think Attucks was angry at British soldiers for taking jobs from the colonists and was there to fight. One account says that Attucks knocked a British soldier down and that's why he was the first colonist shot. However, after the Boston Massacre, Crispus Attucks became a hero to many as a freedom fighter.

Images like this suggest the soldiers fired into the crowd purposefully. It doesn't show colonists attacking the soldiers.

Crispus Attucks

Did You Know?

Not much is known about Crispus Attucks. Some accounts say he led the mob of colonists!

13

THE TRIALS

The British soldiers were put on **trial** for murder. They were **defended** by a great figure in American history—John Adams, who later became the second US president!

Adams was a lawyer who wanted the men to get a fair trial. This was a tough job. During the months after the Boston Massacre, colonists such as Samuel Adams, cousin of John, spread stories of the heroism of the colonists and the wickedness of the soldiers. If the soldiers were found guilty, they would be put to death.

Did You Know?

Samuel Adams used the violence of the Boston Massacre to convince colonists to arm themselves against the British.

Samuel Adams

This image of the massacre shows Captain Preston's arm in the air, commanding the soldiers to fire. Paul Revere was the artist, but one knows if Revere was present that day.

15

WHO SAID "FIRE"?

Captain Preston's trial was first. Did he tell his men to hold their fire? He said he had! John Adams called witnesses to the stand. Some said Preston didn't give the order to fire, while others claimed he did. All agreed many people were yelling at the same time.

Adams pointed out there was no firm proof against Preston. The judge used the famous term "reasonable doubt" for the first time. The **jury** returned a decision of "not guilty."

Did You Know?

Under British law, neither Captain Preston nor his men were allowed to speak at their own trials.

The confusion of the street fight made it hard to prove Captain Preston told the soldiers to fire.

17

THE SOLDIERS' TRIAL

Eight of Captain Preston's soldiers were put on trial for murder in November 1770. John Adams defended them as well. Adams said the angry crowd had made the soldiers fear for their lives. The soldiers were defending themselves and shouldn't be found guilty of murder.

None of the soldiers were found guilty of murder. However, Hugh Montgomery and Matthew Kilroy were found guilty of **manslaughter**. They weren't sentenced to death, but the letter "M" was burned into their thumbs.

Did You Know?

Historians now know that Montgomery admitted to shouting "Fire!" after he was knocked down.

19

AFTER THE MASSACRE

The trial led to more anti-British feelings. As the events were retold by colonists seeking independence, the British were said to be cruel and the crowd were merely blameless victims. Even the name—Boston Massacre—made it sound like many innocent people died.

After the trial, the truth came out that the British officer who bought the wig had paid his bill the day before the violence! What would have happened if Edward Garrick hadn't insulted the soldier? We can only guess.

colonial American flag

Cause and Effects: The Boston Massacre

Cause:

England raised taxes to pay for the French and Indian War.

Effect:

Increased taxes made colonists angry.

Effect:

To keep the peace, soldiers were stationed in Boston, Massachusetts.

Effect:

The soldiers' presence further angered the colonists.

Effect:

A mob surrounded a group of soldiers on March 5, 1770.

Effect:

The soldiers fired into the crowd, killing five men.

Effect:

Colonists' anger over this and other events led to the American Revolution.

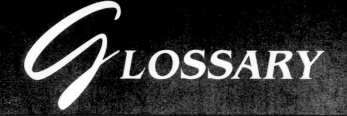LOSSARY

apprentice: one who works under a skilled professional in order to learn an art, craft, or trade

bayonet: a blade that can be attached to the end of a rifle and used for stabbing

debt: money owed

defend: to act as a lawyer for. Also, to drive danger away from.

insult: to say or do something rude that offends someone

jury: a group of people chosen to listen to a legal case and make a decision

manslaughter: the unlawful killing of someone without advance planning

massacre: the killing of a large number of people, especially when they cannot defend themselves

representation: the fact of having someone speak or act on others' behalf, such as in government

revolution: a movement to overthrow an established government

trial: an examination of facts and law in a court to decide an issue

violence: the use of physical force to injure someone

FOR MORE INFORMATION

Books

Benoit, Peter. *The Boston Massacre*. New York, NY: Children's Press, 2013.

Fradin, Dennis Brindell. *The Boston Massacre*. New York, NY: Marshall Cavendish Benchmark, 2009.

Weiss, Lynne. *Crispus Attucks and the Boston Massacre*. New York, NY: PowerKids Press, 2014.

Websites

The Boston Massacre Files
bostonhistory.org/sub/bostonmassacre/game.html
Play a game using the facts of the Boston Massacre.

Boston Massacre Trials of 1770
law2.umkc.edu/faculty/projects/ftrials/bostonmassacre/bostonmassacre.html
Read more about the trials following the violence in Boston in 1770.

*J*NDEX

Adams, John 14, 16, 18, 19

Adams, Samuel 14

American Revolution 4, 5, 21

Attucks, Crispus 12, 13

Battles of Lexington and Concord 4, 5

Boston 4, 6, 9, 11, 21

British soldiers 5, 6, 8, 9, 10, 11, 12, 13, 14, 17, 18, 21

colonies 4, 6

crowd 8, 10, 11, 13, 18, 20, 21

England 4, 6, 21

French and Indian War 6, 21

Garrick, Edward 8, 20

Kilroy, Matthew 18

Montgomery, Hugh 18

Preston, Thomas 10, 15, 16, 17, 18

Revere, Paul 15

snowballs 4, 10

Stamp Act 7

taxes 6, 9, 21

trial 14, 16, 18, 19, 20

wig 4, 8, 20